The Arms of Glastonbury Abbey

Glastonbury Gleanings

An inspirational book about certain
Saints, Kings and Abbots associated
with Glastonbury Abbey,
together with a selection of
prayers and readings

compiled by

F. Vere Hodge, MC
Prebendary of St Decuman's in Wells Cathedral

The Canterbury Press
Norwich

Copyright © F. Vere Hodge, M.C. 1991

First published 1991 by The Canterbury Press Norwich
(a publishing imprint of Hymns Ancient & Modern Limited)
St Mary's Works, St Mary's Plain,
Norwich, Norfolk, NR3 3BH

British Library Cataloguing in Publication Data
Vere Hodge, F.
Glastonbury gleanings: an inspirational book about
certain saints, kings and abbots associated with
Glastonbury Abbey, together with a selection of prayers
and readings.
1. Somerset (England). Abbeys. History
I. Title
942.3830922
ISBN 1–85311–026–4

*Typeset by Rowland Phototypesetting Limited
Bury St Edmunds, Suffolk
and printed in Great Britain by
St Edmundsbury Press Limited
Bury St Edmunds, Suffolk*

FOREWORD

Any visitor to Glastonbury will feel the pull and 'magic' of this special place. Although noted for its legend relating to 'Avalon' and Joseph of Arimathea, the real story of Glastonbury is located in the broken, cast-down Abbey which still projects its evocative shadow into the daylight of today's Church.

Part of the story of the Abbey is revealed in this splendid little book by Prebendary Vere Hodge who is currently Chairman of the Glastonbury Abbey Trustees.

I commend 'Glastonbury Gleanings' with pleasure.

+ George Bath & Wells

October 1990   Bishop of Bath & Wells
                            and Archbishop designate of
                            Canterbury

To

Eleanor, Anthony, David and Felicity

CONTENTS

ACKNOWLEDGEMENTS

I do thank most sincerely all those who have so kindly helped me with the preparation of this book. Naturally I take full responsibility for the presentation of the material, and for mistakes. Whilst every effort has been made to trace owners of copyright material, my sincere apologies are offered for any omissions or errors.

The idea of writing the book began with Dr Robert Dunning, who is Editor of the Victoria County History of Somerset and also a Trustee of Glastonbury Abbey, and who suggested to me that I should write a book which would encompass the Saints of Glastonbury and their prayers. The book which has taken shape is somewhat different from that original conception, but Dr Dunning has nevertheless most kindly helped me in the preparation of it, both with guidance and with subject-matter. His advice has been invaluable: but in fairness to him I must add that there are a few places where I have not taken it.

My warmest thanks go to my Diocesan Bishop, Dr George Carey, for so kindly writing the Foreword when he was snowed-under with work, having just become the Archbishop-designate of Canterbury.

Also, I am most grateful to the following for generously allowing me to use material from their publications: Mr Philip Nokes and the Bath & Wells Diocesan Board of Finance for the Collect for St Dunstan from the Diocesan book *Special Forms of Service*; Mr Vernon Blyth and the Bath & Wells Diocesan Education Committee for extracts from King Edgar's Coronation Service and for St Benedict's times of Services; Basil Blackwell for the Prayer of St Benedict from *Day by Day* by Rowland Purton; Boydell & Brewer Ltd for extracts from William of Malmesbury's writings, edited by John Scott (see Bibliography, p. 52); James Clark & Co Ltd, Cambridge, for 'An Old Glastonbury Collect' from *St Joseph of Arimathea at Glastonbury* by The Reverend Lionel Smithett Lewis; The Covenant Publishing Co. Ltd for the Gildas quotation from *The Coming of the Saints* by J. W. Taylor; J. M. Dent & Sons Ltd for the Riddle from *Anglo-Saxon Poetry* by Professor R. K. Gordon, No. 794 in Everyman's Library; Victor Gollancz Ltd for the poem 'At Milking Time' from *God of a Hundred Names* by Barbara Green and Victor Gollancz; John Murray (Publishers) Ltd for Prayers by King Alfred, St Dunstan, St Ethelwold, St Bernard of Clairvaux and St Brigid, all from *A*

The Abbey Church from the east.

Chain of Prayer Across the Ages by Selina Fitzherbert Fox; The Venerable G. B. Timms for the Collect for St David's Day from *The Cloud of Witnesses* by Martin Draper; and George Weidenfeld & Nicolson for the extract from *The Age of Arthur 350–650* by John Morris. Extracts from the Authorized Version of the Bible (the King James Bible), the rights in which are vested in the Crown, are reproduced by kind permission of the Crown's patentee, Cambridge University Press.

For the illustrations, my special thanks go to Mr Jerry Sampson (photographs on pages x, 5, 29b, 33b, 36, 41, 43 and 45) and Mr Brian Walker (ix, 9, 11, 16, 21, 24, 27, 29a, 31a & b, 35c, 39 and 50), for taking great trouble to produce appropriate photographs. Also to Mr Paul Ashdown (19), The Bodleian Library, Oxford, for MS Auct. F.IV.32 fol. 1^R (17), and Mr Paul Ashdown, The Reverend Douglas Dales and Dr Robert Dunning for the explanation of it; to Professor James Carley, Mr John Loveridge and the Glastonbury Antiquarian Society, and Mr Kevin Redpath (33a); to Mrs Dacre Lacy (37), Mrs Pat Robinson and The Palace Trustees, Wells (35c), and The Reverend P. S. Thomas (35a & b).

I am of course indebted to the authors of the works listed in the Bibliography; and for a variety of kinds of help I am most grateful to Mr Registrar Roger Bird, Mrs Victoria Dawson, Miss Gina Dobbs, The Reverend Charles Hadley, Mr William Hadley, Mr William Hancock, Lieut.-Colonel H. R. Jordan, Mr Wallace Jordan, Mrs Eve Low, Miss Auriol Milford, Miss Pamela Nicholls, Commander Malcolm Scadding, RN, Captain John Shillingford, RN, Miss Mary Siraut, Mr P. C. Stoyle and Staff at Bridgwater Reference Library, Somerset County Council; and The Reverend James Turnbull.

Finally, my most grateful thanks to Mr Kenneth Baker and The Canterbury Press Norwich, for so painstakingly helping me to assemble my material into the format which you now see.

F.V.H.

The Glastonbury Thorn on Wearyall Hill, traditionally the spot where Joseph of Arimathea's thorn staff rooted. There is another Thorn at the Abbey, and one in St John the Baptist churchyard.

GLASTONBURY ABBEY

Somerset, England

An asterisk (*) denotes that a separate entry appears elsewhere in book (see contents page)

The Somerset Tradition is that *Joseph of Arimathea was the Virgin Mary's uncle, that he was a trader who travelled to Britain to buy tin from Cornwall and lead from Somerset, and that on one or more of these voyages he brought the young Jesus with him. And that they built at Glastonbury a little, simple place of worship, a tiny church if you like, of interwoven willow branches plastered with mud: 'the wattle church', often subsequently called 'the Old Church'.

One cannot prove the truth of this by written evidence, but it has been an oral tradition which many Somerset people —and I am one of them—believe is true. In 633 Paulinus, the first Bishop of York, had the little church encased in wood and lead, to preserve it; but it was destroyed in the great fire of 1184.

There are other stories too, about Joseph bringing the Holy Grail—the cup used at the Last Supper—and other relics. I do not know the truth of these; but undoubtedly Glastonbury has been a Holy Place from very early days; and it still retains its own special atmosphere.

Little is known about it during the next two centuries; probably a hermitage or a little group of Christians was established, loyal to the Celtic Church. The Church in Britain had certainly become stabilized by 314, because in that year three British bishops attended a Synod at Arles, in the south of France.

Around the year 500, *King Arthur appears in our misty history, fighting against invading Saxons. He, with his Queen, Guinevere, is said to have been buried in the Abbey churchyard. Many years later, their bones were re-interred in the presence of *King Edward I and *Queen Eleanor.

Arthur's dates are uncertain; but we know that *St Gildas lived in the sixth century, and we are indebted to him for some knowledge of our country's early history.

In the eighth century, *King Ine made gifts of land to the monastery, and of money for the building of a stone church and for the raising of the standard of the Abbey generally. In the ninth century, *King Alfred rose to free the whole south of England from the Danish invaders; and in the tenth, *St Dunstan came on the scene. He tightened up the discipline at the Abbey, and really put Glastonbury on the map. He was assisted by his friend *St Ethelwold, who became Prior of the Abbey.

Dunstan was to exert considerable influence on the Saxon kings of his day. To us, they seem very young: Edmund was about 17 when he came to the throne, Edred 14, Edwy 14 and *King Edgar 16. Edmund and Edgar were buried at Glastonbury Abbey, as subsequently was King Edmund Ironside, about 1016.

King Edward the Confessor, who died in 1066, was not buried at Glastonbury; but the Abbey did achieve some fame on his account because one of the monks, *St Brihtwold, made a remarkable prophecy about Edward's succession to the throne.

A contemporary of Brihtwold, *St Ethelnoth, joined the select band of Glastonbury priests who became Archbishop of Canterbury (in 1005). A century later, *Henry of Blois was appointed Abbot, and substantial building works were carried out during his abbacy.

Twelve years after his death, the Abbey caught fire, on 25th May 1184, and was burned to the ground. Rebuilding began at once, and the first part of the new Abbey to be built was a chapel on the site of the Old Church, the holiest spot in the whole of the grounds; and the new chapel continued the dedication to the Virgin Mary: the Lady Chapel. In due course this chapel became the western end of the new Abbey, whose remains we see today.

It is recorded that a substantial part of the new Abbey was ready by Christmas Day 1213; but building continued, with intermissions, for the next three centuries, many of the Abbots making notable additions to the Abbey Church and ancillary buildings. To represent the 'Building Abbots' I have chosen *Abbot Adam de Sodbury (1323–1334).

The end came in 1539: the Dissolution of the Monasteries under King Henry VIII. On 15th November in that year, *Abbot Whiting and two of his monks, *Brother John Arthur and *Brother Roger Wylfryd, were executed on Glastonbury Tor. The Abbey was sold into private hands, and during the succeeding four centuries the various owners took down the buildings and sold the stone.

Two buildings were left virtually untouched: the small, detached chapel dedicated to *St Patrick, perhaps spared because it served as a chapel for the adjacent alms houses; and the Abbot's kitchen, which provided a refuge for Quakers and Huguenots in the seventeenth century.

In 1907, the Abbey property came on the market, and was bought back by the Church. Since then, the Abbey ruins and grounds have been the responsibility of Trustees appointed by the Bishops of Bath & Wells. It is not the intention to rebuild the Abbey physically, but to build it up spiritually, a source of inspiration for our nation and for the world.

NOTE ON THE SPELLING OF NAMES

Spelling of names can differ considerably; I have recorded some variations in the page sub-headings. In older books, names which I have started with an A or an E (Alfred, Ethelnoth) may often be found under Æ or Ae.

St Joseph of Arimathea
1st century

St Mark[1] describes Joseph of Arimathea as Εὐσχήμων translated as 'honourable' in the Authorized Version of the Bible.
Mark's Greek word means something like 'a true gentleman';
but it also came to be used to mean 'well-off', and Matthew
paraphrases Mark's word in that sense: 'a rich man'.

Other information about Joseph of Arimathea, given in the
four Gospels, is that:

* He was a 'Councillor', probably meaning that he was a
  Member of the Jewish Sanhedrin, the highest court of
  justice and the supreme council at Jerusalem, consisting of
  71 priests and laymen.
* He did not assent to the Council's condemnation of Jesus.
* He was a disciple of Jesus, 'but secretly, for fear of the Jews'.
* He overcame this fear on the day of the Crucifixion in order
  to ask Pilate for our Lord's body.
* Assisted by Nicodemus (the man who had gone to visit
  Jesus by night) he took the body of Jesus from the cross and
  laid it in his own, unused, tomb.

There is no contemporary written confirmation of the
tradition that Joseph of Arimathea brought Jesus to Somerset
when he was a boy (see page 1); but the fact that Pilate
recognised Joseph's claim to our Lord's body on Good Friday
evening implies that Joseph was related to Jesus.

---

[1] Mark 15.43. The other references are Matthew 27.57–60, Luke 23.50–53,
John 19.38–end. See also John 3.1 and Isaiah 53.9.

The HISTORY of that Holy Disciple

JOSEPH of Arimathea,

Wherein is contained,

The true Account of his Birth, his Parents, his
Country, his Education, his Piety, and how he
begged of PONTIUS PILATE the Body of Our
Blessed Saviour, after his Crucifixion, which he
buried in a new Sepulchre of his own.

Also the Occasion of his Coming to ENGLAND,

Where he first preached the Gospel at Glastenbury in
Somersetshire ; and where is still growing that noted White-
Thorn, which buds every Christmas-Day in the Morning,
blossoms at Noon, and fades at Night, on the Place where
he pitched his Staff in the Ground.

With a full Relation of his Death and Burial.

The first page of a six-page 17th century booklet in the Abbey Library.
The pages are so fragile that it is not suitable to display the book.

5

King Arthur

c. 500

Since Mr Leslie Alcock's excavations at Cadbury Castle, Somerset, in the late 1960s, Arthur has become more accepted by historians, and Alcock feels that 'there is acceptable historical evidence that Arthur was a genuine historical figure, not a mere figment of myth or romance'.

Arthur lived in the middle of the Dark Ages: dark because little light is shed on what was happening then, in those hidden years between the departure of the Roman Army and the establishment of a Saxon kingdom, 410 to roughly 600.

Traditionally, he was the son of Uther Pendragon and nephew of Ambrosius Aurelianus, who is an historical British leader who strongly opposed the Saxon invaders. Arthur is credited with a dozen victories against the Saxons; the best attested is the Battle of Badon Hill. Arthur is said to have died at the Battle of Camlann, but the site and date are unknown.

From this point the darkness falls again. Was Arthur (and subsequently his Queen, Guinevere) buried at Glastonbury Abbey?[1] We don't know; but it is by no means impossible, because even then Glastonbury was regarded as a specially holy spot, and at least three of the Saxon kings were to be buried there.

Whatever the truth may be, the story of King Arthur has been linked with Glastonbury Abbey for many centuries. The stories have multiplied, and have been written and related in many tongues. They have been, and still are, a source of inspiration for deeds of chivalry, courage and endeavour throughout the world.

---

[1] see further pages 28–29.

THE KING ARTHUR CROSS

By *Dunstan's time, say 950, the Abbey graveyard was full, so
it was walled round, the principal graves covered with stone
slabs, and then earth carted and deposited to make a second
tier of burials possible.

In 1191, the monks uncovered one of these slabs, and
below it they found what had apparently been an 'important'
burial; and on the underside of the stone was a small leaden
cross. It has unfortunately been lost; but the drawing above
was made by the historian William Camden prior to 1607.

The inscription reads: 'HIC IACET SEPULTUS INCLITUS REX
ARTURIUS IN INSULA AVALONIA', 'Here lies buried the
famous King Arthur in the Isle of Avalon'. The lettering is not
contemporary with Arthur, but could be of Dunstan's time: so
it may be that he had the cross made and positioned.

'Avalon' is a Celtic word meaning 'The Island of Apples',
and in Celtic mythology was used to describe an earthly
paradise set in the western seas. Perhaps by a misunderstanding
of its etymology, in the Arthurian literature Avalon became
identified with Glastonbury, and is still in current use.

The bones which the monks discovered in 1191 were apparently
then moved into the church, and in 1278 were re-interred in the
presence of King Edward I and Queen Eleanor (*see pages 28–29).

St Gildas

c. 480–c. 560

Born probably on Clydeside, Gildas may have married as a young man, and been widowed. In any event, he became a monk, and soon gained respect in Wales where Irish monks used to visit him; and he may have visited Ireland. For some years he used to spend Lent on Steep Holm, an island in the Bristol Channel. He became one of our earliest historians, though a somewhat pessimistic one.

Gildas was a renowned preacher. Caradog of Llancarfan, who wrote a *Life* of Gildas c. 1140, related that his fluency once deserted him when a pregnant woman came into the church: he was so moved that he could not continue, because it came to him that this baby, as yet unborn, was a special child. The woman was St Non, and the child was to become *St David of Wales.

Gildas went for a time to Brittany, to Morbihan Island, near Ruys, where he founded a monastery. There he wrote his *Liber querulus*, 'Book of Complaints' about his own country-men, the British. It contains a reference to how the Christian faith was brought to Britain 'towards the end of Tiberius Caesar's reign'. Tiberius ruled from AD 14 to 37, dates which fit in well with the *Somerset Tradition.

There are two versions of how Gildas spent the last years of his life. One opinion is that he stayed at Ruys and died there. The other, that he returned to Somerset, built a hermitage near Glastonbury, and lived there until his death, when he was buried at the Abbey.

Certainly his Feast Day was commemorated there from early times, at least from the tenth century, on 29th January.

ST GILDAS' WORDS

This is the text, put into modern English, of the passage in Gildas's book referred to on the opposite page:

'These islands [Great Britain] received the beams of light—that is, the holy precepts of Christ—the true Sun, as we know, at the latter part of the reign of Tiberius Caesar, in whose time this religion was propagated without impediment and death threatened to those who interfered with its professors.

These rays of light were received with lukewarm minds by the inhabitants, but they nevertheless took root among some of them in a greater or lesser degree, until the nine years' persecution by the tyrant Diocletian, when the churches throughout the whole world were overthrown.'

The Emperor Diocletian's persecution of Christians began in 303, but may have taken a year or so to reach Britain.

John Morris translates some words of Gildas on Fasting:

'Abstinance from bodily foods without charity is useless. The real *meliores* [the stricter monks] are those who fast without ostentation . . . not those who think themselves superior because they refuse to eat meat . . . or to ride on a horse or in a carriage; for death enters into them by the windows of pride.'

A stone from the shaft of an Anglo-Saxon cross, with symmetrical interlace pattern (on display).

King Ine

(Ina, Ini)
?–726; reigned 688–726

Under the year 688 the Anglo-Saxon Chronicle records the succession of Ine to the Kingdom of Wessex, that he 'reigned thirty-seven winters', and that 'he founded the monastery of Glastonbury; after which he went to Rome, and continued there to the end of his life'.

Ine took a leading part in welding together what had up to this time been mostly isolated monasteries and churches. In civil legislation, he drew together various old laws, added new ones, and consolidated them into a code of law based on Christian principles. This Doom of Ine has influenced our common law to this day.

At Glastonbury, Ine had a new, stone church built, to the east of the Old Church; it was dedicated to St Peter and St Paul. His church was built of 'Tor burrs', large lumps of local stone, an example of which may be seen lying on the south side of the Abbot's kitchen.

As well as the new church for Glastonbury (and probably one for Wells too) it was through Ine that the Abbey gained other possessions, including land on the Polden Hills and in the Zoyland area. This gave the Abbot considerable power over the moor land, leading in later years to some notable clashes between Abbots and Bishops.

King Ine had a long reign, for those days. He successfully beat off many challenges to his authority; but perhaps he was not cut out for warring. In 726 he abdicated, and went to Rome, where he died after a few months. Maybe he would have preferred to make the church his career.

THE DOOM OF INE

King Ine produced the earliest extant code of law for his kingdom, southern England; no doubt he drew on previous laws and practice and added more of his own. King Alfred did the same, two centuries later, adding Ine's code as an appendix to his own laws.

These compilations were known as 'dooms', the 'Doom of Ina' or 'of Alfred' and so on; hence 'Doomsday Book', as it used to be spelt.

Ine's code was essentially practical; for example:

If a slave works on Sunday at his master's command, he is to be free, and the master is to pay 30 shillings as a fine.
If however the slave works without his knowledge, he is to be flogged.

If anyone is liable to be flogged, and reaches a church, the flogging is to be remitted.

Church-scot [a tax for the church] is to be given by Martinmas; if anyone does not discharge it, he is to be liable to 60 shillings and to render the church-scot twelve-fold.

If anyone fights in a minster, he is to pay 120 shillings compensation.

A child is to be baptized within 30 days; if it is not, 30 shillings compensation is to be paid.

Fragment of an early 8th century stone cross (on display).

11

King Alfred

846–899; reigned 871–899

The Viking invaders were pouring over Western Europe, and no leader, not even Alfred's elder brothers, had proved able to stop them.

With great personal valour and tenacity, Alfred did stop them. In the winter of 878/9 he had withdrawn into the Somerset marshes at Athelney (the site of the cake burning story). Picking his moment, Alfred gathered every man he could and came off the moor to beat back the Danish King, Guthrum.

Guthrum agreed to become a Christian, and Alfred stood sponsor to him when he was baptized at Aller, near Athelney. Alfred assigned the northern part of England to Guthrum, and kept the southern part.

The invaders still kept coming; yet Alfred made time to forward the mental and spiritual welfare of the Kingdom as well as defending it physically. He laid the framework of sound government, he improved *Ina's and Offa's codes of law, and he understood the need for education and a cultural heritage. He founded schools, brought scholars over from the continent, and himself translated important Latin texts into the language of his time, Anglo-Saxon.

The Anglo-Saxon Chronicle, under the year 883, records: 'Pope Marinus [or Martin] sent King Alfred the *lignum Domini*' ('Wood of the Lord', that is, a piece of the Cross). The story is that Alfred presented this, or part of it, to Glastonbury's Abbot.

King Alfred died on 26th October 899.

A PRAYER OF KING ALFRED

*Lord God Almighty, Shaper and Ruler of all creatures, we pray
Thee for Thy great mercy, that Thou guide us better than we
have done, towards Thee.*

*And guide us to Thy will, to the need of our soul, better
than we can ourselves. And steadfast our mind towards Thy will
and to our soul's need. And strengthen us against the
temptations of the devil, and put far from us all lust, and
every unrighteousness, and shield us against our foes, seen
and unseen.*

*And teach us to do Thy will, that we may inwardly love
Thee before all things, with a pure mind.*

*For Thou art our Maker and our Redeemer, our Help, our
Comfort, our Trust, our Hope; praise and glory be to Thee
now, ever and ever, world without end. Amen.*

FROM BOETHIUS
One of the Latin authors whom King Alfred translated
into Anglo-Saxon was Boethius. He was a Roman
philosopher, almost contemporary with St Benedict
(c. 470–c. 524) who wrote his principal work while a
political prisoner. This is a short extract from
Alfred's translation, put into modern English:

*O Father, give the spirit power to climb
To the fountain of all light, and be purified.
Break through the mists of earth, the weight of the clod,
Shine forth in splendour, Thou that art calm weather,
And quiet resting place for faithful souls.
To see Thee is the end and the beginning,
Thou carriest us, and Thou dost go before,
Thou art the journey, and the journey's end.*

St Dunstan

c. 909–988

Dunstan was the outstanding product of Glastonbury Abbey as the Abbey became the outstanding product of Dunstan's influence. He was born near Glastonbury, educated at the monastery, took his monk's vows there, was ordained priest in 939 and soon became Abbot. In 959 he was made Archbishop of Canterbury.

In the Church, helped by *Ethelnoth, he succeeded in his aim to impose a strict standard of life, according to the Rule of *St Benedict, on the Glastonbury monks initially but eventually in monasteries throughout southern England.

As a statesman, Dunstan managed to retain the confidence of three out of four of the young Kings, Edmund, Edred and Edgar, and so was able to guide them over some forty years.

And he was a skilled writer, illuminator, metal worker and musician; he designed and had built a number of magnificent organs; and he encouraged and raised the standard of English monastic art.

The psychic side of his nature was well-developed, and caused him to have a variety of 'seeings' throughout his life. Indeed, he seems to have been one of those who live half in this world and half in the next: a gift which does not make for an easy life.

On Ascension Day, Thursday 17th May 988, he preached three times in Canterbury Cathedral. This tired him, and he spent Friday in bed. On Saturday morning he received Holy Communion, and began to sing Psalm 111: 'I will give thanks unto the Lord with my whole heart . . .'. So he died, and was buried at Canterbury. His Feast Day is 19th May.

A CONFESSION AND PRAYER FOR FORGIVENESS, BY ST DUNSTAN

O *Lord*, O King, resplendent in the citadel of heaven, all hail continually; and of Thy clemency upon Thy people still do thou *have mercy*.

Lord, Whom the hosts of cherubim in songs and hymns with praise continually proclaim, do Thou *upon us* eternally *have mercy*.

The armies aloft, O *Lord*, do sing high praise to Thee, even they to Whom the seraphim reply, 'do Thou *have mercy*'.

O *Christ*, enthroned as King above, Whom the nine orders of angels in their beauty praise without ceasing, deign Thou *upon us*, Thy servants, ever to *have mercy*.

O *Christ*, Whom Thy one only Church throughout the world doth hymn,
O Thou to Whom the sun, and moon, and stars, the land and sea, do service ever, do Thou *have mercy*.

O *Christ*, Whose holy ones, the heirs of the eternal country, one and all with utter joy proclaim Thee in a most worthy strain, do Thou *have mercy upon us*.

O *Lord*, O gentle Son of Mary free, O King of kings, Blessed Redeemer, upon those who have been ransomed from the power of death, by Thine own blood, ever *have mercy*.

O noblest unbegotten, yet Begotten Son, having no beginning of age, yet without effort (in the weakness of God) excelling all things, upon this Thy congregation in Thy pity, *Lord have mercy*.

O Sun of Righteousness, in all unclouded glory, supreme Dispenser of Justice, in that great Day when Thou shalt strictly judge all nations, we earnestly beseech Thee, upon this Thy people, who here stand before Thy presence, in Thy pity, *Lord, then have mercy upon us*.

Dunstan built this prayer upon the framework of the 'Kyries', the ancient petitions (in Greek) 'Lord have mercy, Christ have mercy, Lord have mercy', each repeated three times. The Kyries are still frequently used in Christian worship today.

KEY TO THE PICTURE OPPOSITE

It is a drawing of Christ as the Wisdom of God, holding the budding rod of the Kingdom of God and a tablet (or book), with Dunstan at prayer at his feet, on a steep hill, probably Glastonbury *Tor. Above the whole, in a different (15th century) hand are the words: 'Pictura et scriptura huius pagine subtus visa est de propria manu Sci Dunstani', 'Drawings and writings below on this page are in the actual hand of St Dunstan'.

The words in Dunstan's hand are:

Along the rod: VIRGA RECTA EST VIRGA REGNI TUI, 'The sceptre of thy Kingdom is a right sceptre' (Psalm 45 v. 6, AV).
On the tablet: VENITE, FILII, AUDITE ME; TIMOREM DOMINI DOCEBO VOS, 'Come, ye children, hearken unto me: I will teach you the fear of the LORD' (Psalm 34 v. 11, AV). Significantly, this quotation is also in the Prologue to the Rule of *St Benedict.
Above the saint: DUNSTANUM MEMET CLEMENS ROGO CHRISTE TUERE, TENERIAS ME NON SINAS SORBSISSE PROCELLAS, 'Remember, I beg you, merciful Christ, to protect Dunstan, and do not permit the storms of the underworld to swallow me up'.

A stone from the pre-Conquest Abbey (on display).

William of Malmesbury (c. 1130) recorded: 'Dunstan, through whose labour the church blossomed anew, made organs and two notable little bells here, an altar cloth and a bell in the refectory on which are these (words): "Dunstan ordered this bell to be cast for himself"'.

BATH & WELLS DIOCESAN COLLECT FOR
ST DUNSTAN'S DAY

*Almighty God, whose holy servant Dunstan, schooled by thy
grace, restored thy church in violent and careless times: Grant to
thy Church in this and every age leaders and pastors to recall us to
the ancient disciplines and to speak thy Word afresh to doubting
and fainthearted men; through Jesus Christ our Lord. Amen.*

St Ethelwold

c. 912–984

Born at Winchester, Ethelwold was ordained by Alphege, Bishop of Winchester, on the same day as his friend *Dunstan, in 939. He soon joined Dunstan at Glastonbury; both were keen to see monasticism revived in England, and both believed that a strict adherence to the Rule drawn up by *St Benedict was the way to do it.

Ethelwold became Prior of Glastonbury. He rarely slept after matins (about 3.0 am), and ate meat only occasionally. King Edred presently persuaded him to go to build up the decayed monastery at Abingdon.

In 963 he was made Bishop of Winchester, and with the approval of *King Edgar he dismissed the clergy serving the cathedral and replaced them with monks, so establishing the first monastic cathedral chapter in England.

During his time as Bishop, Ethelwold drafted the 'Regularis Concordia', the Agreement concerning the Rule, for English monks and nuns. Based on the Rule of St Benedict, it brought about that revival of monastic life for which he and Dunstan had striven, especially in the southern half of England.

Ethelwold was a practical man. At Glastonbury, he used to cook; and at Abingdon he worked on the buildings until he fell and broke several ribs. At Winchester, he had an organ constructed which had some 400 pipes, 36 bellows, and needed two monks to play it.

St Ethelwold has the reputation of being austere, and a disciplinarian; yet contemporaries could speak of him with affection as 'the benevolent Bishop, the Father of monks'. His main Feast Day is 1st August.

*After a drawing in an 11th century copy of
the Regularis Concordia. The figures represent
St Ethelwold, King Edgar and St Dunstan.*

A CONFIRMATION PRAYER BY ST ETHELWOLD

We beseech thee, Lord, open thy Heavens; from thence may thy
gifts descend on *him*. Put forth thine own hand from heaven
and touch *his* head. May *he* feel the touch of thy Hand, and
receive the joy of the Holy Spirit, that *he* may remain
blessed for evermore. Amen.

King Edgar
943–975

Educated by *Dunstan and *Ethelwold, Edgar became King of all England when he was only 16; but it was not until Whit Sunday 973 that Dunstan, by then Archbishop of Canterbury, crowned him in Bath Abbey. The delay was probably because 30 was considered the suitable kingly (or episcopal) age.

As a young man, Edgar sowed his wild oats rather publicly, his activities including attempts to seduce some of the young nuns at Wilton, near Salisbury. Sister Wulfhilda resisted him, one one occasion having to crawl along a drain to escape him. But he succeeded with Sister Wulf(th)ryth, who bore him a daughter, Edith.

Wulfhilda and Edith both became saints; and despite these escapades, after his death King Edgar was regarded by many people as a saint, although he was never canonized. In fact, in later years Edgar's reign was looked upon as a golden age.

This with considerable justification. One of Edgar's first acts as King was to recall Dunstan from exile, and appoint him to be his adviser, so making possible the close co-operation between Church and State which marked Edgar's reign.

Edgar also strengthened the code of English law, organized a system of coastal defence against Scandinavian raiders and founded some thirty monasteries. For those days, his reign was a peaceful one; when he died at the age of 32, his body was brought to Glastonbury Abbey for burial. About 1500, a chapel named after King Edgar was added to the east end of the Abbey.

He was locally remembered on the day of his death, 8th July.

KING EDGAR'S CORONATION

A tablet on the outside of Bath Abbey reads: *'EDGAR FIRST KING OF ALL ENGLAND WAS CROWNED BY DUNSTAN, ARCH-BISHOP OF CANTERBURY, IN THE SAXON ABBEY ON THIS SITE ON WHIT SUNDAY AD 973'*

A description of that Coronation Service has come down to us from an almost-contemporary source, 'The First Life of St Oswald'.

After the Te Deum, Edgar made these solemn promises:
'First of all I promise that the Church of God and all Christian people shall enjoy true peace under my rule at all times.
'Then I promise to ban all crimes and violence with regard to all sorts and conditions of men.
'Thirdly, I shall command mercy and justice in all my judgements so that the merciful and kindly God may grant His mercy to you and to me.'

There followed the Prayer of Consecration and the anointing with holy oil, accompanied by the words based on I Kings 1, 'Zadok the priest and Nathan the prophet anointed Solomon king', to which the congregation replied 'May the King live for ever'. Dunstan then crowned the King, and invested him with ring, sword, sceptre and orb.

So the pattern of Service in 1953 was closely similar to that used in 973. It remains a potent symbol of that partnership between Church and State which was so carefully fostered by King Edgar.

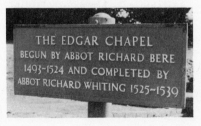

The Edgar Chapel was the last part of the Abbey to be built, at the east end.

St Ethelnoth

?–1038

Not every Archbishop of Canterbury in a difficulty can claim to have had his King jump out of his bath and come to help; indeed, maybe not all our kings have had baths to jump out of. But this did happen to St Ethelnoth.

Ethelnoth was a Glastonbury monk who in 1020 was made Archbishop of Canterbury. He became a trusted adviser to King Cnut, who helped the Archbishop with various church projects, and also gave valuable benefactions to Ethelnoth's old monastery, Glastonbury.

The bath incident happened when Ethelnoth appealed to the King for help to steal Archbishop Alphege's body from St Paul's Cathedral and carry it to Canterbury: euphemistically known as the 'Translation' of St Alphege, who had succeeded *Ethelwold as Bishop of Winchester and had been made Archbishop of Canterbury in 1005.

The King had Royal servants posted outside St Paul's to deter objectors, while two monks opened St Alphege's tomb. They seem to have been singularly disorganized, because they had to use an iron candlestick as a crowbar, and when they got the body out on to a plank, they had to take an altar dust cloth to cover the corpse. This was then ferried across the Thames in the Royal barge, and escorted to Canterbury.

Cnut delegated considerable power to Ethelnoth. He was called 'The Good', and the Anglo-Saxon Chronicle has the entry: '1038 This year died Ethelnoth, the good Archbishop' adding 'and, within a little of this time, Bishop Ethelric in Sussex, who prayed to God that he would not let him live any time after his dear father Ethelnoth; and within seven nights of this he also departed'. St Ethelnoth is remembered on the anniversary of his death, 30th October.

I have not been able to find a writing of Archbishop Ethelnoth; but here is a rhyme attributed to his friend, King Cnut.

Cnut went one year in a barge to Ely, to keep the Feast of the Purification of the Blessed Virgin Mary (2nd February). As the barge approached Ely, the sound of the monks singing came over the water. The King told his men to listen; and he made up this song:

> Merie sungen (th)e muneches binnen Ely,
> Da Cnut ching reu (th)er by;
> Rowe(th) cnichtes noer (th)a land,
> And here we (th)es muneches sæng.

CNUT AND THE TIDE

King Cnut's rebuke to his scycophant courtiers used to be well-known, but as it is now nearly always completely misrepresented, I give the outline of it here:

As Cnut was walking along the shore with some courtiers one day, some toadies began to flatter him, saying 'Not only England obeys you, but Denmark, Norway and Sweden too; in fact, you are so powerful that if you ordered the tide to stop coming in, it would obey you'.

Cnut was annoyed by this silliness, and to show the speakers what nonsense they were talking, he called for a chair, sat facing the sea, and ordered the tide not to encroach further on his land. When the tide did not obey, Cnut turned to the courtiers and said: 'Oh! foolish men, do you not know that to God alone belongs such power. He alone rules earth and sky and sea, and we and they alike are His subjects, and must obey Him'.

St Brihtwold

(Brihtwald, Berhtwald)
c. 975–1045

Lord Peter Wimsey, referring to the statement in the Prayer Book marriage service that 'such persons as have not the gift of continency might marry', said that he 'wouldn't have it as a gift'. History has not recorded the comment of Edward [the Confessor] when he heard that one of the Glastonbury monks, Brihtwold, had seen a vision of St Peter crowning him (Edward) King of England, and at the same time granting him a life of celibacy.

We do not know Brihtwold's early history, but in the year 1005, while he was still a Glastonbury monk, he was chosen and consecrated to be Bishop of Ramsbury, near Marlborough. Ramsbury was the see for the diocese of Wiltshire and Berkshire, created in 909 out of the over-large diocese of Winchester. It existed for only a century-and-a-half, because Brihtwold's successor, Herman, had the see moved to Old Sarum. (In 1974 it became suffragan to Salisbury).

Brihtwold served at Ramsbury for forty years. But he seems to have felt cut off from the monastic life, and probably went back to Glastonbury when he could. He gave many substantial gifts to Glastonbury Abbey, which caused some mutterings among his flock, some of whom thought that he took too much out of the Diocese, to give to Glastonbury.

Brihtwold died on 22nd April 1045, and was buried at Glastonbury Abbey. He must have been at least 30 (the minimum age) when he was consecrated bishop, which makes him 70 when he died. His Feast Day is 22nd January.

Fragment of carved Anglo-Saxon stonework (on display).

BRIHTWOLD'S GIFT

William of Malmesbury, writing about Glastonbury
in the 1130s, relates that Brihtwold gave 'the three
shrines of the Saints Guthlac, George and Oswald,
on which are the following verses:

'The humble priest, Brihtwold by name,
To the Highest Lord and His mother Mary,
Grants this small gift with a devout heart,
Committing it to the old church of Glastonbury
So that he may win the sweet delights of eternal life.'

A RIDDLE

Long before the invention of the crossword, our Saxon forbears
used to enjoy riddles. This one has been put into modern
English (with the solution at the end) by Professor R. K.
Gordon.

I know a noble guest cherished in his excellent dwelling, whom
grim hunger cannot harm nor hot thirst, old age nor illness. If
the servant tends him kindly, he who must ever go on the journey,
they shall find in safety in their home food and gladness appointed
for them, countless kindred; sorrow, if the servant obeys his lord
badly, his master on the journey. Nor will one brother fear
another; when, hasting away, they both leave the bosom of one
kinswoman, mother and sister, they both suffer. Let the man who
will, set forth in fitting words what the stranger is called or the
servant of which I speak here.

The answer
'The noble guest' is the soul; its servant and brother is the body. The earth is
mother and sister to both—mother, because man's body is made from her;
sister, because she was made by the same father—God.

25

Henry of Blois

?–1171
Abbot of Glastonbury 1126–1171,
Bishop of Winchester 1129–1171

Grandson of William the Conqueror and younger brother of King Stephen, Henry of Blois at first supported Stephen when the Empress Matilda challenged him for the English throne. Later, Henry went over to Matilda, and then back to Stephen; yet still managing to remain for over forty years both Abbot of Glastonbury and Bishop of Winchester.

Henry was a young monk at Cluny when his uncle, Henry I, instructed him to come to England to be Abbot of Glastonbury. Henry was horrified to find the run-down state of the Abbey; the buildings were dilapidated and the monks' living conditions poor.

The right man had been sent to pull Glastonbury up. Henry organized proper meals, and set about putting the buildings to rights. Although he was soon made Bishop of Winchester, as well as remaining Abbot, he appointed efficient Priors at Glastonbury to take charge during his absences.

Henry restored, or built anew, the dormitory, refectory, infirmary, lavatory, chapter house and cloisters. He improved the library, and added rich furnishings in the church.

In 1131 Henry I granted Henry and future Abbots the right to hold an annual three-day Fair, from the Feast of Our Lady's Nativity (8th September): an important privilege for both Abbey and town.

Impetuous and autocratic, perhaps; but Henry of Blois was a man who battled on for his Abbey and his Diocese. He was Vicar-of-Bray-ish, but that was probably to his peoples' advantage. His final twist was actively to promote the Treaty of Wallingford, which gave the Throne of England to Matilda's son, Henry II.

*This is a carving on blue lias stone, probably
from the cloister arcade which Henry of Blois
built.*

*The sharpness of the carving, 800 years
later, is remarkable. Probably the stone fell
during the great fire of 1184, and became
buried until it was refound in the 20th
century; so the detail of the design has
been preserved. (On display.)*

A PRAYER OF ST BERNARD OF CLAIRVAUX,
a contemporary of Abbot Henry of Blois:

Deliver us from our enemies, we beseech Thee, and
defend us from all dangers to soul and body, that
at length we may come to Thine eternal rest;
through Jesus Christ our Lord. Amen.

King Edward I and Queen Eleanor

1239–1307   ?–1290
Reigned 1272–1307

We said that *King Arthur was 'a source of inspiration for deeds of chivalry, courage and endeavour'; and one of the men whom his story inspired was King Edward I. Edward early proved himself an efficient as well as a brave fighter, and he saw himself the successor to Arthur as King of All Britain.

He was fortunate in marrying a wife who matched him: Eleanor of Castile. When he sailed for Syria as a Crusader in 1271, she insisted upon accompanying him; and when he was stabbed with a poisoned dagger, she sucked the poison out of the wound.

Edward's interest in Arthur may account for his co-operation when the Abbot of Glastonbury invited him to come to the Abbey for the dedication of the new High Altar and the reinterment of the bones of King Arthur and Queen Guinevere, in 1278.

The King and Queen arrived in Glastonbury for Easter. On Easter Tuesday, 'Arthur's' tomb was ceremonially opened, to reveal two chests painted to represent Arthur and Guinevere. The bones were taken out, and King Edward wrapped up those from the Arthur chest, and replaced them. Queen Eleanor performed the same service for the bones in the Guinevere chest. The two skulls and the knee joints were kept out to be shewn as relics.

John of Glastonbury, writing around 1350, records that when the bones were replaced, the tomb was directed 'to be placed speedily before the high altar'. The removal of the High Altar eastwards in 1368 accounts for the distance between the site of the Altar and the site of the tomb today.

ON THE DEATH OF KING EDWARD I

All that are of heart true,
A while hearken to my song
Of douleur that death hath dealt us new
That maketh me sigh and sorrow among;
Of a knight that was so strong
Of whom God hath done His will:
Methinks that death hath done us wrong
That he so soon shall lie still.

All England ought to know
Of whom that song is that I sing;
Of Edward, king that lieth so low,
Through all the world his name did spring
Truest man in everything,
And in war wary and wise,
For him we ought our hands to wring,
Of Christendom he bare the prize.

Though my tongue were made of steel,
And my heart smote out of brass,
The goodness might I never tell
That with King Edward was.
King, as thou art called conqueror,
In each battle thou hadest the prize;
God bring thy soul to the honour
That ever was and ever is
That lasteth aye without end,
Pray we God and our Lady
To that bliss Jesus us send.

*Part of a head, carved
in white lias stone;
14th century
(on display).*

—*Author unknown
(Granger's Index to Poetry)*

SITE OF KING ARTHUR'S TOMB.
IN THE YEAR 1191 THE BODIES OF
KING ARTHUR AND HIS QUEEN WERE
SAID TO HAVE BEEN FOUND ON THE
SOUTH SIDE OF THE LADY CHAPEL.
ON 19TH APRIL 1278 THEIR REMAINS WERE
REMOVED IN THE PRESENCE OF
KING EDWARD I AND QUEEN ELEANOR
TO A BLACK MARBLE TOMB ON THIS SITE.
THIS TOMB SURVIVED UNTIL THE
DISSOLUTION OF THE ABBEY IN 1539

*Notice by the site of
the Tomb, in the choir.*

Adam de Sodbury

?–1334; Abbot 1323–1334

Before becoming Abbot, Adam had held two responsible posts at Glastonbury Abbey, Sacrist and Cellarer. As Sacrist, he was responsible for the Communion vessels and linens, and as Cellarer for catering supplies and general stores for the monastery.

Adam was a good manager, and during his eleven years as Abbot he improved the living conditions of the monks and at the same time put the Abbey's finances on a sound footing. He greatly improved the Abbey Church too, having most of the nave vaulted, and the nave walls painted with pictures of saints, kings and heroes. He built chapels dedicated to St George and St Sylvester; and it was probably he who removed the wall between the Lady Chapel and the Galilee, so making the Abbey a single building from the west end of the Lady Chapel to the east end of the choir.

Adam had bells cast and installed in the central tower and also in a detached campanile; he had a new organ built, and a new clock constructed. A story was put about that it is this clock which is now in Wells Cathedral: but that is not so. Gold and silver for decoration, and fine altar cloths and hangings were some of Adam's other generous gifts to the Abbey.

He also helped the parishes which the Abbey served, helping with the sea-wall near East Brent, building several village churches and having windmills erected to help Shapwick and Meare.

When Adam died, he was buried in the nave: probably one of the first to be buried within the church; and his parents were buried either side of him.

'OUR LADY'S SONG': 14th century

Iesu, swete sone dere!
On porful bed list thou here,
And that me greveth sore;
For thi cradel is ase a bere,
Oxe and asse beth thi fere:
   Weepe ich mai tharfore.

Iesu, swete, beo noth wroth,
Thou ich nabbe clout ne cloth
   The on for to folde,
   The on to folde ne to wrappe,
For ich nabbe clout ne lappe;
Bote ley thou thi fet to my pappe,
   And wite the from the colde.
               —*Anonymous*

[bere = byre, fere = friend,
lappe = fold of garment, wite = keep]

*Contemporary stone head,
carved in blue lias (on display).*

*Medieval stone coffin found beneath the paving almost in
the centre of the crossing in the Abbey Church (on display).*

Abbot Richard Whiting

The last Abbot of Glastonbury: c. 1476–1539

On 15th November 1539 Abbot Whiting and two of his monks (*see page 34*) were taken to the steep hill on the edge of Glastonbury, the Tor, and there hanged.

Richard Whiting was probably born in Somerset, Wrington way, and may have attended school at Glastonbury Abbey. He became a monk at the Abbey, was made deacon in 1500 and priest in 1501. On the death of Abbot Bere in 1525, Cardinal Wolsey appointed him to be Abbot.

Abbot Whiting inherited considerable responsibilities: the care of the monks and the Community, care for the parishes round about which the Abbey served, the management of the extensive properties and possessions of the monastery, and of the monastic school, and the obligation to entertain benefactors and visitors.

There was no suggestion that Abbot Whiting did not carry out his duties faithfully. But in 1539 the end came. He was 'tried' on a charge of concealing some of the Abbey's treasures; there was also some vague charge about a book he had written against the King's divorce, but that was not produced. The real point was that the great Benedictine Abbots—Glastonbury, Reading and Colchester—had to be destroyed.

After the execution, Abbot Whiting's head was placed over the Abbey's western gateway, on Magdalene Street, and his quartered body displayed in Wells, Bath, Ilchester and Bridgwater. The shock to Glastonbury and for Somerset and beyond must have been tremendous.

Abbot Whiting was Beatified by the Roman Catholic Church in 1896, bestowing the title 'Blessed'. Locally, we remember him and his monks often, but especially on 15th November.

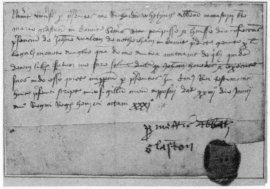

A receipt signed by Abbot Whiting, 'Ric Abbatt Glaston' (on display in The Tribunal, High Street, Glastonbury).

THE EXECUTION

As Abbot Whiting and his companions were taken to their execution, they must have had in mind some of our Lord's words, as St John recorded them. The Abbot probably thought of them in Latin: this is the English version published by William Tyndale, who was himself strangled and burned at the stake three years before Abbot Whiting's execution.

John 16.1–4
These thinges have I sayde vnto you, because ye shuld not be offended. They shall excommunicat you: ye the tyme shall come, that whosoever killeth you, will thinke that he doth God service. And suche thinges will they do vnto you, because they have not knowen the father nether yet me. But these thinges have I tolde you, that when that houre is come, ye myght remember them, that I tolde you so.

Glastonbury Tor.

The 13th century tower of St Michael's church witnessed the killing of Abbot Whiting and the two brothers (see p. 34).

Brother John Arthur
Brother Roger Wylfryd
?–1539

These were the monks who were executed with Abbot Whiting on 15 November 1539.

'Arthur' and 'Wylfryd' were their names given when they took their vows: before that, they were John Thorn and Roger James. The 'given' name was usually chosen by the monk after somebody whom he admired; often after someone previously associated with their monastery. 'Arthur' was obviously after King Arthur, and 'Wylfryd' was presumably after St Wylfryd, Bishop of Northumbria, who had given land to the Abbey.

Brother John Arthur was Treasurer of the Abbey. It is his name which is associated with the well-known 'Glastonbury chair' (*illustrated on the next page*).

Brother Roger Wylfryd, the Sub-Treasurer, was one of the youngest monks. He and Brother John were hanged one on either side of Abbot Whiting, and the thought of the Crucifixion must inevitably have been in their minds—and surely in the minds of everyone present.

As the two Brothers and their Abbot were taken to their ignominious deaths, the pillaging of the Abbey began. Perhaps it had become rather too rich, and too powerful; and we have the opportunity now not to rebuild it physically, but to concentrate upon rebuilding the Abbey as a spiritual centre, a spiritual power-house and force for good in our country and world-wide.

Both Brothers were Beatified with their Abbot (*see page 32*), and are remembered locally particularly on 15th November.

TWO CHAIRS

In the Bishop's Palace at Wells are two chairs associated with Glastonbury Abbey. One is the bobbin chair on which Abbot Whiting sat during his 'trial' in the Great Hall of the Palace.

The less well known chair pictured here, from Kingweston Church, is also associated with Abbot Whiting, and one of the back panels is carved with a crozier and the initials R.W. The final stroke of the W. has been broken off.

The chair appears to have been altered and mended; but the two vertical back panels may well be contemporary with the Abbot.

The other chair was apparently made by Brother John Arthur, perhaps after a design brought back from Rome by Abbot Bere about 1504. The Latin inscription carved on the chair reads:

JOHANES ARTHURUS · MONACUS GLASTONIE · SALUET EŪ DEUS · SIT LAUS DEO · DA PACEM DOMINE

which may be translated:

JOHN ARTHUR · MONK OF GLASTONBURY · GOD GIVE HIM HEALTH · PRAISE BE TO GOD · GIVE PEACE O LORD

This chair was given to a former Bishop by descendants of Abbot Whiting's sister. The design has been widely copied down the years, and is still made in Glastonbury High Street by Mr Gordon Browning.

Interior of St Patrick's Chapel

ABBEY WORSHIP TODAY

Members of all recognized Christian denominations are welcome to conduct Services in the Abbey, by prior arrangement. There is a Service of Holy Communion every Tuesday at 10.30 am (except Christmas Day); although it is conducted according to the Anglican rite, all Christians are invited to participate.

There are also annual Pilgrimages, and many visits for worship and prayer by groups and by individual people. A special area has been set aside in the grounds and is managed as a wildlife sanctuary, so that the non-human Creation may have its representatives (plants, insects and small mammals) in the Holy Place.

The monks' work was 'opus dei', 'God's work'; and that is what we should all strive to be doing.

Some more elusive Saints

We now come to St Patrick, St Bridget and St David, three Saints who have long been associated with Glastonbury, although it is uncertain whether they ever came here. They may well have done so; people did travel long distances to visit Holy Places.

Next, St Benedict, because the monks of Glastonbury lived under his Rule at least from the time of *St Dunstan.

Finally, a pot-pourri of Saints whom we know little about, or little about their connection with Glastonbury, but whom it would have been sad to leave out. All these, in their different ways, gave inspiration to the monks and so influenced the life of the monastery.

This design, on a hassock in St Patrick's Chapel, is from the crest of a cast-bronze bell-shrine made about 1100 to house St Patrick's bell, known as The Bell of the Will, and itself almost 700 years old in 1100. The birds and the vine represent resurrection and eternal life.

The hassock design is a reminder both of the Celtic missionaries, for ever on the move spreading the Word of God in the country-side at the bell's summons, and also of the strong tradition of St Patrick's personal links with Glastonbury, of which the Chapel is tangible evidence.

St Patrick

c. 390–c. 461

Born somewhere on the west coast of Britain, Patrick was captured by Irish pirates while he was still a boy, and spent six years in slavery. Then he was either freed or managed to escape, and after various vicissitudes seems to have rejoined his family.

During his adventures, his thoughts had turned towards the Church, and it was now that he became a priest. About 440, the Pope sent him to Ireland, where he became the first Bishop of Armagh. He set about evangelizing the district and organizing the Irish church on a diocesan plan.

Several of Patrick's writings survive: his 'Confessio' (autobiographical), a letter to Coroticus (protesting against the slave trade) and the best-known, 'Lorica', 'St Patrick's Breastplate'.

After the Reformation, two buildings escaped the destruction of the rest of Glastonbury Abbey: the Abbot's kitchen, and the small detached chapel known as St Patrick's. The embroidery designs on the hassocks in the chapel are all taken from Irish works of art in the early days of the church. The name 'Patric' on them is so spelt because the Irish language has no 'k'. The kneeler on the Altar step is taken from a representation of Christ's robe at his crucifixion, 'the hem of his garment' (*Matthew 9.20 and 14.36*). See plaque in shop.

St Patrick's Feast Day is 17th March. But there is an interesting entry in the Abbey's ancient Calender: 'Patrick' is listed under 24th August. This was probably the Feast Day of St Patrick the Older, whose relics Glastonbury possessed; hence possible confusion.

PART OF ST PATRICK'S BREASTPLATE

I bind unto myself today
The strong name of the Trinity,
By invocation of the same,
The Three in One, and One in Three.

I bind unto myself the power
Of the great love of Cherubim;
The sweet 'Well done' in judgment hour;
The service of the Seraphim,
Confessors' faith, Apostles' word,
The Patriarchs' prayers, the Prophets' scrolls,
All good deeds done unto the Lord,
And purity of virgin souls.

I bind unto myself today
The virtues of the star-lit heaven,
The glorious sun's life-giving ray,
The whiteness of the moon at even,
The flashing of the lightning free,
The whirling winds' tempestuous shocks,
The stable earth, the deep salt sea,
Around the old eternal rocks.

Christ be with me, Christ within me,
Christ behind me, Christ before me,
Christ beside me, Christ to win me,
Christ to comfort and restore me,
Christ beneath me, Christ above me,
Christ in quiet, Christ in danger,
Christ in hearts of all that love me,
Christ in mouth of friend and stranger.

—Translated by Mrs Alexander
(1818–1895)

*The north doorway
into St Patrick's
Chapel.*

St Bridget of Ireland

(Brigid, Brigit, Bride)
c. 453–c. 525

Bridget was probably born at Faughart, near Dundalk, Louth.

Singularly little is known about her life. While still young, she apparently became a nun, and founded the first nunnery in Ireland, of which she became Abbess, at 'Cill-Dara', 'The Church of the Oak', now Kildare.

Bridget is associated with work for the sick, and with various miracles, several on the theme of multiplication of food when it was needed. She is thought to have kept animals, hence the common representation of her with her cow. Stone carvings of a woman milking may be discerned on St Michael's tower on Glastonbury Tor, and on the north portal of the Lady Chapel, at the Abbey.

Bridget is revered as the Patroness of poets, healers and blacksmiths. Her biographers, having few facts to record, have had to rely on their imagination. One detail which seems likely to come under this heading has a highly topical theme: it relates how Bishop Mel, of Ardagh, a disciple (possibly nephew) of St Patrick, consecrated Bridget as Bishop. Others say that it was Bishop Ibor who consecrated her.

The medieval association of Bridget with Glastonbury included the dedication to her of a chapel at the Beckery (on the outskirts of the town), and the veneration of several of Bridget's possessions left at the Beckery after a visit.

Whatever the true facts of Bridget's life may be, she is much-loved, and is considered to be the second Patron Saint of Ireland. A number of ancient churches in England and Wales are dedicated to her, the best-known being St Bride's in Fleet Street, London. Her Feast Day is 1st February.

A PRAYER OF ST BRIGID

We implore Thee, by the memory of Thy Cross's hallowed and most bitter anguish, make us fear Thee, make us love Thee, O Christ.　Amen.

*A woman milking: a carving on the tower of
St Michael's Church, Glastonbury Tor.
(There is a similar carving on the north portal of the Lady Chapel,
at the Abbey, on the right-hand side.)*

'AT MILKING TIME'
Bless, O God my little cow,
　Bless, O God, my desire;
Bless Thou my partnership
　And the milking of my hands, O God!

Bless, O God, each teat,
　Bless, O God, each finger;
Bless Thou each drop
　That goes into my pitcher, O God!

—A Gaelic prayer

St David of Wales

died 589 or 601

Few details of David's life are known. His home county was apparently Pembrokeshire (now Dyfed, after him), and there are some ancient church dedications to him there.

An Irish *Catalogue of the Saints* (c. 730) records that David (also Gildas and Teilo) celebrated Mass in Ireland; and a century later an Irish book of martyrs noted David's Feast Day as 1st March.

There is a two-fold connection with Glastonbury. One is an unproven statement that David established ten monasteries, of which Glastonbury was one. He might have reformed Glastonbury; and there is a story that he intended to dedicate the *Old Church to the Blessed Virgin Mary, but our Lord told him in a vision that he had already done this.

The other connection concerns a jewel. It is said that when David visited the Holy Land, the Patriarch of Jerusalem gave him a magnificent stone, known as 'the sapphire'; and that on his return to Britain he presented this to Glastonbury Abbey.

Certainly there was a notable stone at the Abbey, because at the Dissolution it was itemised as 'a Super altare, garnished with silver and gilte and parte golde, called, the great Saphire of Glasconberye'.

In the tenth century, the British were fighting the Welsh in the Menevia (St David's) area, and Glastonbury claimed that a lady named Aelswitha acquired David's bones and brought them to Glastonbury for safety. The Welsh were totally unconvinced, and continued to display their own set of bones.

St David's Feast Day is still 1st March.

ST DAVID
in niche above the
High Altar in Wells Cathedral

COLLECT FOR ST DAVID'S DAY

Grant, O Lord, that as we give thanks for the life and work of
your servant David, so your Church in Wales may faithfully
preach the Gospel which he proclaimed, and build on the
foundation which he laid; through Jesus Christ our Lord.

—The Venerable G. B. Timms

St Benedict

c. 480–c. 543
Patron Saint of Europe

Benedict was born at Nursia, Italy, and studied at Rome; but soon left to live a solitary life at Subiaco. Disciples joined him there, but something went wrong and he moved to Monte Cassino, whose monastery was the scene of a famous Second World War battle.

There Benedict completed his 'Regula Monachorum', 'Rule for Monks'. He called it 'A very small Rule for beginners': his great achievement was to produce a monastic way of life which was moderate and capable of being put into practice.

Alongside the daily round of Services, Benedict planned that each monk should have his work outside the church building, whether cooking, cleaning, gardening, fishing, writing, illuminating or visiting the sick. The resulting Rule came to be widely accepted as the main monastic Rule in the west.

One of the two parish churches in Glastonbury is now called 'St Benedict's' (formerly St Benignus's).

Looking back fourteen centuries, Benedict comes across as an unusual character: a loner, and yet not excessively austere; rather, sensitive to the normal shortcomings of his fellowmen, and careful in his Rule not to lay upon them burdens too heavy for them to bear. He was friendly with the natural creation too, and had a pet raven which used to share his meals with him.

Benedict was buried at Monte Cassino, in the same grave as his sister, St Scholastica. His Feast Day has long been 21st March, the day he died; but since 1969 the Roman Calendar has changed his date to 11th July (his translation).

BENEDICTINE SERVICE TIMES

In his Rule, Benedict set times for the Services of daily worship.
The night was reckoned from 6.0 p.m. to 6.0 a.m., and the day
from 6.0 a.m. to 6.0 p.m. (as in the Bible—and as on modern
electric time clocks). On this plan, Prime was the first Service
each day (as distinct from night), and Terce (Tierce), Sext and
None were, as their names suggest, at the third, sixth and ninth
hours of the day: $6 + 3 = 9$ a.m., $6 + 6 = 12$ noon, and $6 + 9 = 3$ p.m.

Together with the other 'Offices', as these Services are
called, plus two celebrations of the Mass or Holy Communion,
the following formed the order of Services for ordinary days:

Nocturns	2.0 a.m.	Sext	12.0 noon
Matins	3.0 a.m.	None	3.0 p.m.
Prime	6.0 a.m.	High Mass	4.0 p.m.
Terce	9.0 a.m.	Vespers	6.0 p.m.
First Mass	10.0 a.m.	Compline	7.0 p.m.
			or sunset

A PRAYER OF ST BENEDICT

O Gracious and Holy Father, give us wisdom to perceive thee;
intelligence to understand thee; diligence to seek thee;
patience to wait for thee; eyes to behold thee; a heart to
meditate upon thee; and a life to proclaim thee; through
the power of the Spirit of Jesus Christ our Lord. Amen.

St Benedict's Church,
Benedict Street, Glastonbury.

'AND WHAT SHALL I MORE SAY?
for the time would fail me to tell . . .'

. . . the stories of Saints Deruvian and Phagan, how they were sent to Britain by Pope Eleutherius (c. 180), and how they came to Glastonbury and repaired the *Old Church.

Or of St George, probably a Roman soldier who, while stationed at York (c. 300) is said to have made pilgrimage to Glastonbury; and later to have returned to Rome and interceded with Emperor Diocletian to cease his persecution of those following the Christian Way. (Not a recommended method of forwarding one's promotion.)

Or of St Beon, a disciple of St Patrick, who came to Glastonbury and built himself a hermit's cell at nearby Meare, where he lived until his death; and of how, many years later, his remains were brought by boat to Glastonbury for reburial, and how a church was built where his bones were landed. A church which, through a confusion of names, was called after St Benignus (St Benen), and which was later replaced by the existing church, dedicated to St Benedict.

Or of St Kea (Quay), St Fili and St Rumon, Glastonbury monks in the fifth century, who set out to carry the Gospel into Devon and Cornwall, and eventually to Brittany. St Kea's name still exists, hidden, in a part of Street, next to Glastonbury. Once 'Lantocai', 'Church of Kea', it is now 'Leigh'. His Cornish settlement is still called Kea, near Truro. Sixth century St Collen, Patron and Founder of Llangollen Church, Clwyd, is said to have come to Glastonbury too, and Colan in Cornwall is named after him.

Or of St Indracht and his companions, who were murdered at Shapwick, near Glastonbury, about 710. Indracht was probably an Irishman, perhaps of royal birth, who, with his sister, had made a pilgrimage to Rome. They returned via Britain, and visited Glastonbury; and only a few miles away were set upon and killed. Their bodies were taken back to the Abbey for burial.

Or of St Neot (died c. 877), another Glastonbury monk, whose advice used to be sought by King Alfred to whom Neot was related. Because he was short, he had a trivet made which he could carry about, to stand upon. Like St Kea, he too moved to Cornwall and founded a community. He died and was buried there, and the parish is still called St Neot. His name also continues in St Neots, Cambridgeshire.

All these and others were venerated at Glastonbury, and were a source of inspiration to the whole Community . . .

'. . . Wherefore seeing we also are compassed about with so great a cloud of witnesses, let us lay aside every weight, and the sin which doth so easily beset us, and let us run with patience the race that is set before us, looking unto Jesus the author and finisher of our faith; who for the joy that was set before him endured the cross, despising the shame, and is set down at the right hand of the throne of God.'

Hebrews 12.1–2

AN OLD GLASTONBURY COLLECT

recorded by The Reverend Lionel Smithett Lewis,
former Vicar of St John the Baptist, Glastonbury.

Almighty, everlasting God, Who didst entrust Thy most blessed servant, Joseph, to take down the lifeless body of Thine Only-Begotten Son from the Cross, and to perform the due offices of humanity, hasten, we pray Thee, that we, who devotedly recall his memory, may feel the help of Thine accustomed pity, through the same, Our Lord. Amen.

FEASTS AND ANNIVERSARY DATES
of people mentioned in this book

JANUARY	3	St Phagan (Fugatius)
	22	St Brihtwold (Berhtwald)
	25	St Paul (also sometimes with St Peter on 29 June)
	28	King Henry VIII died at midnight, 1547
	29	St Gildas
FEBRUARY	1	St Bridget of Ireland
	2	Purification of The Blessed Virgin Mary (BVM)
	8	King Ine (died ? 727)
	9	St Teilo
	10	St Scholastica
	28	St Oswald
MARCH	1	St David
	3	St Non
	12	St Alphege, Bishop of Winchester
	17	St Joseph of Arimathea (Glastonbury: 31 July) St Patrick
	21	St Benedict (or 11 July)
	25	The Annunciation of the BVM
APRIL	11	St Guthlac
	19	St Alphege, Archbishop of Canterbury
	23	St George
MAY	8	St Indracht
	14	St Deruvian (Dyfan, Damian), or 26 May
	19	St Dunstan
	21	St Collen
	26	King Edmund died, 946 (*See also St Deruvian, above*)
JUNE	29	St Peter, sometimes with St Paul
JULY	2	Visitation of the BVM
	6	King Henry II died, 1189
	7	King Edward I died, 1307
	8	King Edgar died, 975
	11	St Benedict (or 21 March)

	31	St Joseph of Arimathea at Glastonbury (*see also 17 March*) St Neot
AUGUST	1	St Ethelwold
	8	St Beon Abbot & Bishop Henry of Blois died, 1171
	20	St Bernard of Clairvaux
	24	St Patrick the Older (?)
	30	St Rumon
SEPTEMBER	8	Nativity of the BVM: Glastonbury Fair
	9	St Wulfhilda King William I died, 1087
	10	Empress Matilda died, 1167
	16	St Edith
	29	St Michael & All Angels
OCTOBER	1	King Edwy died, 959
	12	St Wylfryd
	13	St & King Edward the Confessor
	25	King Stephen died, 1154
	26	King Alfred died, 899
	30	St Ethelnoth
NOVEMBER	5	St Kea (Quay)
	9	St Benignus (Benen)
	11	St Martin
	12	King Cnut died, 1035
	15	Abbot Richard Whiting and Brothers John Arthur and Roger Wylfryd
	23	King Edred died, 955
	28	Queen Eleanor [of Castile] died, 1290
	30	King Edmund Ironside died, 1016
DECEMBER	1	King Henry I died, 1135
	31	St Sylvester

* * *

St Fili, whose Feast Day is unknown, is
remembered at Glastonbury on St Dunstan's
Day, 19 May.

THREE PRAYERS

for Glastonbury Past, Glastonbury Present and Glastonbury to Come

For Glastonbury Past

Heavenly Father, we remember before you those who have lived and worked and worshipped in this place in past years.

> We give you thanks for their goodness;
> ask your pardon, if need be, for their shortcomings,
> your healing, if need be, for their hurts,
> and your blessing upon them now.

We ask this in the Name of your Son, Jesus Christ our Lord. Amen.

Stone decoration in blue lias, probably from the cloisters which Abbot Henry of Blois built.

For Glastonbury Present

Lord Jesus Christ, we pray for Glastonbury Abbey and for
Glastonbury Town:
—for those who come as Pilgrims, that here they may find
    food for the spirit, and the beauty of holiness;
—for those who come as Visitors, that they too may be
    touched by this Holy Place and find solace in trouble,
    healing in infirmity disorientation or addiction, peace
    in their minds and joy in their hearts;
—for the Members of Staff at the Abbey: the Gatekeepers, the
    Groundsmen, the Cleaners, the Manageress of the Shop and
    her Staff, the Custodian and Office Staff;
—for Members of the Abbey Development Trust: the Trust
    Executive, Treasurer, Fund Raiser, Secretary and helpers;
—for the Abbey Trustees and Abbey Development Trustees;
    for the Clergy and Laity who maintain the weekly Service,
    who organize the Pilgrimages, who arrange the Chapel
    flowers, who act as Guides or as summer Chaplains, and
    who tend the Wildlife Area and the Ducks;
—for the Warden and Staff of Abbey House, the Diocesan
    Retreat House;
—for the Mayor and Mayoress of Glastonbury, and the Town
    Council;
—for all who live in Glastonbury, and for all who work here.

Lord, we commend them to your safe keeping, and ask your
blessing upon them all. Amen.

Glastonbury to Come

Holy Spirit, we pray that you will open the hearts and minds
of the men and women of Glastonbury in the years ahead to
enjoy the wonder and the mystery of the Holy Place in their
midst.
    May they tend it and reverence it, and teach their
children to do the same; so that both Abbey and People may
be prepared for that great Day when the Lord will come to
Glastonbury for the second time.

We ask this in His Name, Jesus Christ our Lord. Amen.

51

BIBLIOGRAPHY

The Age of Arthur 350–650 by John Morris (Weidenfeld & Nicolson, 1973).

The Anglo-Saxon Chronicle translated by The Reverend James Ingram (J. M. Dent & Sons: Everyman's Library No. 624, 1934).

Anglo-Saxon England by Sir Frank Stenton (OUP: Oxford History of England, Volume II).

The Archaeology of Somerset edited by Michael Aston and Ian Burrow (Somerset County Council, 1982).

Arthur's Britain by Leslie Alcock (Penguin Press, 1971).

The Book of Saints by The Benedictine Monks of St Augustine's Abbey, Ramsgate (A. & C. Black, 1966).

Christianity in Somerset edited by Dr Robert W. Dunning, FSA (Somerset County Council, 1976).

The Coming of the Saints by J. W. Taylor (The Covenant Publishing Company).

The Dictionary of Catholic Biography by J. J. Delaney and J. E. Tobin (Robert Hale, 1961).

The Dictionary of National Biography (OUP).

Dunstan: A Handbook for the Millenium by Paul Ashdown (privately printed, 1987).

Dunstan: Saint & Statesman by The Reverend D. J. Dales, BD (Cambridge —Lutterworth, 1988).

The Dunstan 1000 Project by Vernon H. Blyth, Adviser in Religious Education, Diocese of Bath & Wells. (Diocesan Education Committee, 1988).

The Early History of Glastonbury. An Edition, Translation and Study of William of Malmesbury's *De Antiquitate Glastonie Ecclesie*, by John Scott (The Boydell Press, 1981).

Glastonbury by The Reverend C. L. Marson (The George Gregory Book Store, Bath, 1925).

Glastonbury Abbey by Professor James P. Carley (The Boydell Press, 1988).

King Arthur's Avalon by Geoffrey Ashe (Collins, 1957).

Lives of the Saints by The Reverend Professor Alban Butler (1711–1773), revised by H. Thurston and D. Attwater (Burns & Oates, 4 vols, 1953–54).

The Oxford Dictionary of Saints by D. H. Farmer, FSA (OUP, 1978).

St Indract & St Dominic by G. H. Doble (Somerset Record Society, lvii, 1942, 1–24).

St Joseph of Arimathea at Glastonbury by The Reverend Lionel Smithett Lewis (James Clarke/Lutterworth Press, 1922).

The Saxon Age by A. F. Scott (Croom Helm, 1979).

INDEX

Main references are indicated in bold type

DATE DUE

#45220 Highsmith Inc. 1-800-558-2110